THEN & NOW

SHEFFIELD S8

D1322339

Greenhill, Heeley, Meadowhead, Norton, Woodseats

ald
Print

Alistair Lofthouse & Alison Swift

© Alistair Lofthouse & Alison Swift 2009

Printed and published by:
ALD Design & Print
279 Sharrow Vale Road
Sheffield S11 8ZF

Telephone 0114 267 9402
E:mail a.lofthouse@btinternet.com

ISBN 9-781-901587-81-4

First Published August 2009

Many of the photographs used in this book are from *www.picturesheffield.com* from where you may order prints using the reference number on the bottom right of each picture.

You can view/order our entire range of books through our secure on-line ordering system on:

www.printanddesignshop.co.uk

Introduction

The area of Sheffield known as S8 is extremely varied, from the industry and terraced housing at Heeley to the former rural areas of Greenhill that were part of Derbyshire until 1934. Included in this book is the busy shopping area of Woodseats and Sheffield's largest green space, Graves Park.

Bordering Derbyshire at Meadowhead was Sheffield's first airfield, confusingly called Coal Aston Airfield. Established in 1915 by the then Royal Flying Corps it provided a base for number 33 Squadron in defending Sheffield against the Zeppelin threat. It later grew into a large aircraft repair depot and even prisoner of war camp covering much of Meadowhead, but today not a trace of this base can be found.

The famous Sheffield artist and sculpturer Francis Chantry (1781-1841) was born in the area, although he moved to London where he gained fame and wealth for his chiselled busts of famous people. He insisted that upon his death he be buried in Norton churchyard. He was knighted by William IV in 1835 and gives his name to a local pub and street.

There have been a fair few fine houses in S8, many of which still exist such as The Oaks, Norton Hall, Norton Grange and of course, Bishops House which is open to the public.

Beauchief Abbey

Founded in the 11th Century, Beauchief Abbey's land once included the Abbeydale Industrial Hamlet. The Abbey also owned other properties including three corn mills, a fulling mill (for woollen cloth) and an iron smithy. The monks owned the rights to make charcoal in the surrounding woodland. It has also been used as a smithy and for smelting lead. Beauchief Abbey and cottages are often referred to on early maps as the Lodge.

Abbey Lane/Bocking Lane roundabout

In the above picture note the tram, the tram poles and the 'Dr Who' style Police box. The tram service along Abbey Lane was started in 1928 and ran until 1959.

S12818

Abbey Lane Roundabout
Looking north from Bocking Lane, after 1960 as by this time the trams have gone.

Bocking Lane being built.

The name is derived from an old field name, Bocking Fields. This is believed to have come from a person called Bocking or Bockin who is listed in the Norton Hearth Tax Assessment for 1670.

T01708

S12799

Abbey Lane
The junction of Abbey Lane and Chesterfield Road, Trams 416 and 157. I wonder if that's the fishmonger stood outside his shop with the lady looking towards the camera.

S12796

Abbey Lane, Woodseats
This is one of those scenes where a hundred years have gone by with not much change, the main difference being the road.

S16657

Tram Terminus, Abbey Lane
Tram No. 181 at Chesterfield Road and Abbey Lane junction. No 948 Chesterfield Road, Mr John Codd, the Wheelwright is on the right.

The Abbey, Abbey Lane, Woodseats

The Abbey Hotel, No 348 (later renumbered No 944) Chesterfield Road at the junction with Abbey Lane. Formerly an old coaching inn situated on the Chesterfield to Sheffield road, well used by steel traders, farmers and millers.

Chesterfield Road

Woodseats looking towards Abbey Lane and The Abbey pub (which can be seen behind the poplar trees). The road is much wider today and you wouldn't want to walk in the middle of it now!

Woodseats Road approaching Abbey Lane
The garage on the left has recently been re-developed into flats. Above, the old tram pole lampposts are in the process of been replaced by more modern concrete lights.

S02421

School House, Woodseats
Cammell's School, Chesterfield Road, bottom of Cobnar Road. It is still used as a nursery today.

S10524

Ye Olde Sweete Shoppe, 874 Chesterfield Road

The road widening covers the site of this shop today. KFC is probably the nearest building to the site.

Woodseats House, Chesterfield Road
The home of Johnathan Booth, where John Wesley preached his first open air service.

The Big Tree, Woodseats

I have been reliably informed that this is the third 'big' tree here. The first, pictured above was destroyed by a circus elephant. The travelling circus stopped at the pub and tied the elephant to the tree. This was during a bad storm and when the thunder struck, the elephant bolted taking the tree with it. It was later replaced, but had to be removed in the 1980s due to Dutch Elm disease. The third tree is pictured below.

Bingham Road, Woodseats

Cobnar Gardens in the background has since been replaced by modern houses. Named after James Bingham of *Linley, Linacre and Bingham*, steel and file manufacturers.

S22151

The Woodseats Hotel

Parts of this building may date back several centuries. Paranormal phenomena have been recorded here over the years resulting in tennants in the early 1990s having the rooms blessed.

S16476

Chesterfield Road Tram Terminus

George Barker the Confectioner is in the background. Building is taking place, visible just behind the tram. This terminus was temporary until the area was developed and the tramway was extended further.

Tram Terminus

Chesterfield Road and the latest tram terminus by the Chantrey Arms. The pub is named after Francis Chantrey the famous artist and sculptor who was born at Norton and is now buried in Norton church yard.

Chesterfield Road

Another view of the terminus at Chantrey Road including trams 121 & 215 before the bank was built.

Woodseats
Today the Bank still remains and note the very tall telegraph poles. Woodseats has been a busy shopping area for over 100 years.

S08089

Woodseats Palace, Chesterfield Road

The Woodseats Palace was built in 1911 and had seating for 500 people. A balcony was added in the 1930s. Currently a pub it has, in the past, been used for religious services.

S01336

Scarsdale Methodist Church

December 1940 and the church is suffering from blitz damage. Although repaired the building is no longer a church. The Co-Op have also vacated the building on the right.

T01565

Chesterfield Road at bottom of Woodbank Crescent
The site of the old Woodseats Tram Terminus before the tram lines were extended.
The road is much wider now resulting in property to the left losing some of its land.

S01334

Shops on Chesterfield Road, by the end of Meersbrook Park Road
Air raid damage from the Blitz of December 1940. It is interesting to see how some properties were repaired and others not.

Valley Road Meersbrook

Above, F. Colley & Son, Meersbrook Tannery, corner of Valley Road and Chesterfield Road complete with chimney. The building known as Meersbrook Buildings is now multi-use with flats at the rear and shops to the front. The corner shop was for many years a Natwest Bank.

Heeley Electric Palace, London Road

Heeley Electric Palace was opened on the 7th August 1911and seated 1450 people. Converted to sound in 1930 it became part of the Star Group on 20th January 1955. First closed in March 1963, reopening as a Star Bingo Hall. Destroyed by fire in early 1980s the site was then used as car dealership until acquired in 2000 by Ponsfords who extended their shop on to the site. The Jubilee bridge, which connects the two sites, is designed to resemble train carriages.

S03612

Oak Street, Heeley

Marking the end of war in Europe on the 8th May 1945, bunting, flags and perhaps a few parties! Today no domestic property is on the road, a dramatic change showing how local communities have changed since the Second World War. The road derives its name from a belt of oak trees that were nearby.

Sheaf Bank, Heeley
The above photo is from the 1950s, today just the railway and the old chapel remain.

Derbyshire Lane, top of Scarsdale Road
The Cross Scythes Inn, Derbyshire Lane, looking towards Norton Lees Lane. The pub was rebuilt in 1939.

Bagshawe Arms
Previously the New Inn. In the 19th Century there was a Petty Sessions courtroom over the stables to the left of the pub. The Norton Home Guard met here during the Second World War. The pub gets its name from the Bagshawe family who owned

Bishops House

The only surviving wooden house in Sheffield, Bishops House was built in the 16th century. It was named after the sons of William Blythe, John, Bishop of Salisbury & Geoffrey, Bishop of Coventry & Lichfield. It was bought in 1753 by William Shore. It opened as a museum in 1976.

Old Bishops Cottage Sheffield. JWM

S05444

The Norton Hotel, Meadowhead

For many years this was a Berni Inn, one of three in the city with another on Orchard Lane and third at Castle Market, very popular in the 1970s!

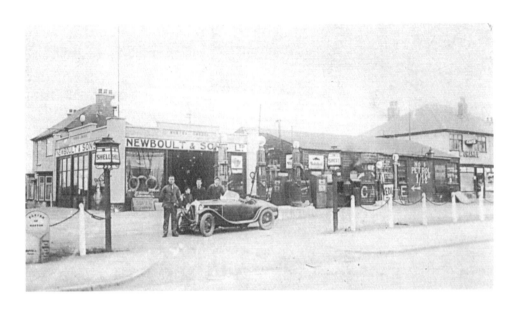

Meadowhead
Newboult's Garage, today still a garage but part of BP. Mentioned on page 39 on the
AA Register of Landing Grounds for the 1930s.

AERODROME, COALASTON NEAR SHEFFIELD.

Norton Airfield

To confuse matters the First World War airfield at Norton was called Coalaston Airfield. RAF Norton, a couple of miles East of here, was never an airfield just a base for barrage balloons used in Sheffield's defence from the Blitz, closing in 1965.

Norton Airfield

Flying started in 1916 from Norton as the Royal Flying Corps 33 Squadron operated from here to defend Sheffield from Zeppelin attack. Soon afterwards the airfield became a major aircraft repair depot under the name No.2 (Northern) Aircraft Repair Depot, RFC Greenhill, Sheffield. After the war civil flying took place here until 1936. Sheffield Council did consider siting an airport on the site! G-AANE 1934 Desoutter Mk1 stands on the airfield.

THE A.A. REGISTER OF LANDING GROUNDS.

 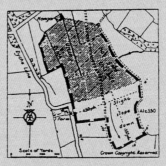

1. CONTROLLED BY The Sheffield Corporation.

2. NO PERMIT IS NECESSARY TO USE THIS AERODROME.

3. SURFACE. Grass and slightly uneven. Liable to be very soft when wet.

4. WARNING. Pilots should not land or take off on the area shaded on the plan, and should only taxi over this with the utmost care.

5. TELEPHONE. Woodseats 45391. Kenning's Garage. Woodseats 45122. Newboults & Son's Garage.

6. FUEL. Aerodrome Garage. Situated at the Cross Roads just by the aerodrome.

7. TRANSPORT Kenning's Garage. (200 yards.) Newboults & Sons. (200 yards.)

8. HOTELS. IN SHEFFIELD. ****Grand, Leopold Street, T.N. 21001. (3½ miles.) ****Royal Victoria Station, T.N. 20031. (4 miles.)

9. RAILWAY. Beauchief Station, L.M.S. (3 miles.)

10. AIR MESSAGE SERVICE BOXES. 22 miles S.W.   37 miles N.

11. NEAREST EQUIPPED CIVIL AERODROME. To Woodford, 29 miles W. 271° True.

12. INSPECTION. First of every month.

| SHEFFIELD. | YORKS. | Y.B. |

An extract from the AA Register of Landing Grounds 1930 relating to Sheffield Airfield

Norton Airfield
A De Havilland D.H.9 stands beside one of the large aircraft hangers. I wonder if the stones below by the football pitch are from this building?

Norton Hall

Once the home of Charles Cammell, one of Sheffield's great industrialists whose empire extended from steel to shipbuilding. It was then owned by Mr Goodcliffe until purchased by Mr B Firth around 1905 who allowed the Army based at Meadowhead to use it for officer accommodation. Recently converted to apartments.

Norton Hall

The Colonnade, once used by the Jessop Hospital for Women, for student training in gynaecological care by Sheffield Hospitals. Norton Hall was built in 1815 by Samuel Shore. Following the failure of the Parker-Shore Bank in the 1840s it was sold to Charles Cammell.

Norton Grange
Built in 1744 for Mr Lowe, Non-Conformist minister to the Offley family of Norton Hall. It Became a Boy's Boarding School, run by the Reverend Henry Piper, from 1814-1833. Occupants included William Fisher.

The Oakes, Norton

Owned for many years by the Bagshawe family it was purchased in 1998 by The Oaks Trust, a registered charity who restored the building to provide a holiday centre for children aged 8-18 years. Their aim is for children to "hear a Christian message, be encouraged in their faith and have a good holiday." All work was funded by donations and almost all the work was carried out by volunteers. Sir Francis Chantrey designed the terrace.

Greenhill Manor

With all the development around it, Greenhill Manor is not as imposing as it once was, however the ornate lamp remains after all these years!

Greenhill Main Road
Old Methodist Church on the right. Politically, Greenhill was in the historic ward of Derbyshire until 1934. In the 12th Century the name is recorded as Greenhilhey.

Millhouses Park
The park was gifted to the people of Sheffield by Earl Fitzwilliam and Marquis of Zetland in 1909. The remainder of the land was purchased by Sheffield City Council. Zetland is an archaic spelling of Shetland. The above pool was replaced by the Lido in the 1960s which was closed in 1980s and below is now just a play area.

Millhouses Park
Bridge in Millhouses Park, over the River Sheaf which today is no longer there. The bridge over the railway, where Millhouses station was, is visible in the background.